BREAKING
THE CHAINS

BREAKING THE CHAINS

Godfrey Rust
Poems & Performance Pieces

WORDSOUT

BREAKING THE CHAINS

First published in Great Britain September 1992.

ISBN 0-95202-120-X

Scripture quotation on page 113 taken from the HOLY BIBLE, NEW INTERNATIONAL
VERSION. Copyright © 1973, 1978, 1984 by International Bible Society.

Cover design by Simon Gunn.   11/11/92

Published by Wordsout Publications, 8 Cleveland Road, London W13 8AU.
Telephone 081 998 4284.

Printed and bound in Great Britain by Clays Ltd., St Ives plc.

UK trade distribution by Word (UK) Ltd., Milton Keynes, England.
Word Australia, Kilsyth, Victoria, Australia.
Word Communications Ltd., Vancouver, B.C., Canada.
Struik Christian Books (Pty) Ltd., Maitland, South Africa.
Christian Marketing New Zealand Ltd., Havelock North, New Zealand.
Jensco Ltd., Hong Kong.
Joint Distributors Singapore — Alby Commercial Enterprises Pte Ltd., and
Campus Crusade.
Salvation Book Centre, Malaysia.

92 93 94 95 / 10 9 8 7 6 5 4 3 2 1

CONTENTS

FOREWORD

This is a book which lives up to its title. Links that join poetry to esotericism, religion to irrelevance and familiarity to contempt are all broken. The collection is crafted without compromise and yet remains accessible. It touches real-life subjects, including religion, with sensitive relevance in such a way that each reading whets the appetite for more.

Godfrey and I have worked together for the last ten years fronting a five-piece musical group. In this context I have watched him perform *Miracles*, introduce *Mischief* and point the way to *The Place Where Socks Go* all in the course of an evening. Despite knowing many of the poems by heart I remain a fan. I never tire of hearing them or sharing the audience's pleasure as they enter the experience for the first time.

The link between familiarity and contempt is broken in so many ways it's worth exploring. Let *A Modern Wife*, for example, reveal her permissive feelings. The language is familiar. The rhythm is easy. You think you've understood, but she still has a few nagging questions which won't let you go.

What could be more familiar than having a baby, celebrating Christmas, or going to work? Look through the eyes of the poet and you will find yourself saying "I never saw it like that before."

What is true of the poetry is also true of the man. The more I have come to know Godfrey the more I have appreciated his faithful friendship and creative character. Like many artists he has a melancholic streak, but unlike so many he has a humility which sometimes underestimates his achievements. Being a husband, father and businessman means that varieties of reality blend together in his poetry.

Sail the Ark with him and you will find an honest man facing his own questions. Listen to *Herod's Last Request* and you will be encouraged to make your own. Look for the *Squiggles* and you may have to go back to square one. It's not all comforting but it is stimulating, which after all is the reason for the rhyme.

If I had to name a favourite it would be *Teddy Bears*. I suppose because beginnings can be difficult and journeys confusing I enjoy a happy ending. No doubt you'll choose your own.

These poems are meant to be available. This book, I hope, will enable many more to enjoy what I and others have enjoyed over the years. Read them to yourself. Read them to others or even read them to an audience. In this way I know you will enjoy the experience of *Breaking the Chains*.

GEOFF SHATTOCK
July 1992

ACKNOWLEDGEMENTS

These poems were written between 1980 and 1992. Some were published in a previous collection *The Place Where Socks Go* or have appeared in magazines and anthologies. Many are printed here for the first time.

Some of the later and longer pieces, including the Christmas poems, the meditations *Peace* and *The Word's Out*, and the title poem, were written for events at St John's Church, West Ealing.

Thanks are due to friends, especially Geoff Shattock, James and Mary Lazarus and Jackie Searle, for their encouragement in believing these poems are worth wider circulation; to Judith Dakin without whose frequent (unpaid!) commissions at St John's many would not have been written; to Simon Jenkins, Noël Halsey, Linda Finley-Day, Alison Jenkins and Win Kennedy for their suggestions and help beyond the call of duty in the production of this book; and last and most to my wife Tessa for her love, support and patience.

ADAM

it wasn't me

it was that woman
she doesn't know what's good for her
she did it

and then
it was that snake
horrible slimy snake
I wouldn't have believed a word
I wouldn't have been taken in
imagine a talking snake
well I ask you

and then
and then
it was you
you made Eve
you made the serpent
it's your rotten apple
you knew all about it —
I was miles away
doing the garden like I was told

you're the one
you did it
it wasn't me
it *wasn't* me

and anyway I only took a little bite

MISCHIEF

In the beginning
God made physicists
out of nothing at all.

"Now hold on"
said the physicists,
"that's against a law."

God,
having not yet made Newton,
said nothing.

Then God made theologians
and became man
and joined them.

"Oh no" said the theologians,
"it's one thing or the other,
God or man."

God smiled
and passed the bread and wine.

Finally God made philosophers
and died for them.

"We've got you there"
said the philosophers.
"Immortals don't die — it's inconsistent!"

But God,
having anticipated this objection,
got up,
packed away his shroud
and walked back into town to see his friends.

And then
just when he'd got them really interested,
just when then they were running out of arguments,
just when it looked like he'd put them straight
once and for all,
God made disciples
and left.

But that's God for you,
always full of surprises,
never know what he won't do next.
Wouldn't put it past him
just about now
with the physicists, theologians and philosophers
thinking they've almost worked it out
to come back
and prove them wrong again —

even though
it's the very last thing
he's likely to do.

NUCLEAR FAMILY

It wasn't so much a fall
as a fallout.
Eve split the apple
and started a Cain reaction
which no one was Abel to stop.

None has since escaped the sickness —
see how the children glow!
Beneath achievement's blossoming cloud
we measure out our half-lives,
radiant with sin.

THE PLACE WHERE SOCKS GO

There's a place where socks go
    when the washing is done
and the driers have dried
    and the spinners have spun
and it's past eight o'clock
    and there's no one about
and the launderette's locked —
    then the odd socks come out.

There is hosiery here of
    each pattern and hue —
some plain, striped or spotted,
    some black, red or blue —
some worn only once,
    some so old they have formed
to exactly the shape
    of the foot they once warmed —

some were brought back from Sock Shops
    in airports in France,
some were hideous presents
    from matronly aunts —
but in all their variety
    one thing is shared:
to the place where socks go
    they will not go pre-paired.

Then the odd socks remaining
 are placed in the chest
(*They must turn up sometime* ——
 now where was that vest . . .?)
and new socks come at Christmas
 and birthdays bring more
and the old lie, alone,
 at the back of the drawer.

And maybe, one evening
 when memory is low,
they too slip away
 to the place where socks go
and in silent reunion,
 each one with its pair,
they join in the dance
 with the other things there ——

the letters unanswered,
 the calls not returned,
the promises broken,
 the lessons not learned,
the lost afternoons,
 the appointments unmade,
the best of intentions,
 the debts never paid,

and the friends not kept up
    and the others let down —
in the ragbag of conscience
    they waltz sadly round,
beyond the respite
    of the washing machine,
no amount of detergent
    can now get them clean

till that day when all laundry
    is washed white as snow,
and everyone's tumbled
    and soft soap must go,
when nothing is hidden
    but all is revealed
and socks shall be holy
    and souls shall be healed.

REVISED VERSION

Don't need my Bible any more.
I've got my daily paper.
They have so much in common.

On page 1
both name the Sun,
and differ only
on the identity
of the owner.

On page 2
both have strong opinions
on man's behaviour,
and differ only
(in the interests of fairness)
in that the serpent
is now given equal space
to put his view of things across,

and on page 3
both saw that they were naked,
and differ only now
in the fixed smiles
and the total collapse
of the fig-leaf market.

A Modern Wife

We grew up in the Sixties
when everything was new.
We only stopped at nothing
when nothing was taboo.
So who put up this barrier
that I cannot break through?

We had an open marriage.
We lived and we let live.
I never asked for anything
he didn't want to give.
So what is it we both resent
and neither can forgive?

We gave the kids their freedom
because it was their right.
They had the information.
They had the appetite.
So who is it I think I've failed
when they stay out all night?

We never hid our feelings.
We had no place for sham.
We freed ourselves to be ourselves.
We didn't give a damn.
So why is it I lie awake
and wonder who I am?

JOSEPH AND THE SHEPHERDS

Midnight in Bethlehem, Zero AD.
One or two people in difficulty.
Out on the street with a donkey and wife
Joseph had reached a bad point in his life
with the kind of a problem that won't go away:
a woman in labour, and nowhere to stay.
Now the root of it all, when you boiled the thing
    down,
was too many people in too small a town.
When they dreamed up the plan of administration
for a poll tax on all of the Jewish nation
only a bureaucrat somewhere like Rome
would send everyone back to their ancestors' home,
for little old Bethlehem wasn't designed
to cater for David's prolific line.
Still the problem was there and he couldn't
    disown it:
they'd left it too late, and Joseph had blown it.
If they'd finished the packing the evening before,
and not gone back to check that they'd locked the
    front door —
if they'd not missed the turning at that
    roundabout —
if they'd filled up the donkey before they set out —
if they hadn't agreed to call in and see
all of Mary's relations at Bethany —
or if only he'd booked by Israeli Express
that would have done nicely. But this was a mess.
No room at the inn. No room anywhere.
They gave him the only place they could spare
and the promised Messiah was born that night
on the floor of a stable without any light
where they cut the cord and cleaned up the mess
and wrapped him in somebody's workaday dress

and while Mary slept there, exhausted and cold,
Joseph sat by feeling helpless and old.
This wasn't the way he had thought it would be
when the angel had told him that destiny
chose them to look after the Holy One.
No, this was a farce. What God had done
was to trust the care of the Saviour instead
to a man who could not even find him a bed.
If only he'd planned it more carefully then.
If he only could go back and do it again.
He turned round in his mind the way he had
    blundered —
then he looked at the infant and suddenly wondered
if it all was a lie, if he was a fool
and the object of everyone's ridicule,
if the dreams of the angels were tricks and not
what they promised to be, and his anger grew hot
when the shepherds burst in all breathless and wild
and stopped in their tracks when they saw the child.
They shifted their gaze from the baby's bed
and their eyes met his, and he nodded his head,
standing awkwardly, not knowing quite what to do
now they all knew for certain the story was true.
They stayed there for minutes. It might have been
    years.
Not one of them spoke. Their hopes and their fears
were gathered around this helpless God
as their minds tried to grasp what it meant. Where
    he stood
Joseph was silent as finally
he saw this was how it was planned to be,
that the smell and the dark and the dirt and the pain
were not Joseph's mistake but God's choice. As the
    rain
ran down on Bethlehem Joseph knew

that men would be saved despite all they might do.
He could not control it. He did not understand.
He felt like a baby himself in God's hand.
He thought of his anger and flushed now with
    shame.
He remembered the angel had said that his name
would be Jesus, God saves.
                         He glanced up and saw
that the shepherds had gone. Day had dawned.
    From the floor
Mary looked at him, quizzical, on her straw bed.
The tiny God-child cried out to be fed.
Joseph moved to the business of the new day,
gave the child to its mother, the donkey some hay.

THE APPEAL

Good evening. May I speak to you
about the little you can do
to contribute towards the health
of someone who can't help themself.
I'm sorry that it's such a bore.
You've seen them many times before —
these harrowing, pathetic scenes,
the faces on your tv screens
with staring eyes and hollow cheek
from playing squash three times a week.
Their diets bring them ever closer
anorexia nervosa,
their freezers swollen and distended —
this cannot be what God intended.
Their tap-water's undrinkable:
they buy Spa by the bottleful
and suffer quite beyond endurance
the ravages of health insurance.
They lack even the will to fight
the despot ruler, appetite,
or raise the least dissenting voice
against the tyranny of choice.
Pity those who can afford
the luxury of being bored.
This is the end of the appeal.
These problems are unbearable.
Send no money. What we need
is millions less mouths to feed.
Please carry on just where you're lying.
Don't let us interrupt your dying.

RONEO AND JULIET

We met in the
Xerox copy shop,
each looking for
enlargements.
Her face
was my type
and I hoped she might
duplicate
my feelings,
but while I had it down
in black and white
it soon became transparent
she brought only
a handful of
negatives,

so seeing
there could be no
developments
I left,
wondering if
some day her
prints will come
prints will come
prints will come
prints will come
prints will come

EVE

Every time
   I get to the bit
  where the serpent

                         sidles up to Eve

   telling the most blatant lie

I always think
    This time she won't fall for it
         not this time
         not our Eve

and every time
   I get to the bit
  where she takes the fruit
        (turning it lovingly in her artless fingers,
           stomach hollow with desire)

I always think
    DON'T DO IT
       surely this time she won't do it

but she does

every time, damn it
she does

MIRACLES

I don't believe in miracles.
There's always a rational explanation.

I believe
the Red Sea was parted
by a rockslide
coming at a convenient time
(though not convenient of course
if you happened to be Egyptian).

The five thousand were fed
by long French loaves
which they had selfishly
hidden up their jumpers
and which the Gospel writers carelessly
omitted to mention.

The water wasn't turned into wine exactly,
it was more God's way of saying
Water's very nice too, you know.

The healings weren't anything remarkable.
Jesus was just a good doctor
a bit ahead of his time,
say about 10,000 years.

As for the Virgin Birth,
I've always thought
that sort of thing just
inconceivable,

and Jesus didn't really rise.
His disciples just wanted
to keep the truth alive,
so they stole the body
and lied about it.

I don't believe in miracles.
There's always a rational explanation.

RIOTS BY REEBOK, BLOOD BY BENETTON

The young today
have one parent,
two pairs of trainers
and a three-second attention span.

Sorry, did you miss that?

The young are consumers
of sex, television and hamburgers,
sometimes, for convenience,
all at the same time.

They think the world
owes them a living.
Unfortunately
it is seriously overdrawn.

The young don't know they're born.
So they keep fighting to get out.

The young have got it made.
So all they can do now
is take it to pieces again.

Don't be afraid of them.
They're only living
up to the expectations
in which they were raised.

The young today
have the world at their feet,
so they kick its brains out
in fits of designer rage,

missing parts
easily replaced
at any branch
of Body Shop.

THE OPTIMIST EXPLAINS

Of course
we must do
everything we can
to keep people alive

so that one day
someone may find out
why
we must do
everything we can
to keep people alive

THE JOURNEY OF THE MAGI (CONT.)

Coming as they did from the first century
they had a few problems with London traffic
and were seriously misled by signs
to the Angel and Kings Cross.

Inquiring diligently about the star
they were referred to Patrick Moore,
who hadn't actually seen God
but would keep an extra eyebrow raised.

In Harrods
the camels made a mess
all over soft furnishings.
On the Underground
commuters glared at No Smoking signs
as incense wafted gently through the carriages.

And when the great day came
they saw the entire voting population
slumped on sofas by four o'clock,
rendered senseless by too much
dead poultry and the Queen,
while over Liberty's and Hamley's
the flickering angels sang
Glory to God in the High St . . .

. . . and they found him
(with the inns full up again)
in the old familiar place,
bringing their unregarded gifts
to the empty stable of the human heart
where the infant Christ is born
again and again and again.

Synod

The atmosphere was generous,
the speeches made with care,
the viewpoints all were fully heard,
the vote was free and fair,

and outside in the corridor
God waited patiently
to find that he existed
by a clear majority.

THE DANGERS OF THEOLOGY

Where the apostles (fortunate of men
to understand your mysteries!) had then
only you, Holy Spirit, to draw on
we have concordance and the lexicon,
such commentaries and textual critiques
that keep our curates occupied for weeks
as verse by verse they plumb divinity.
The angels, awed, stand dumbly by as we
religiously apply the apparatus
(each new translation failing to placate us),
prod at your secrets, first this way then that,
as schoolchildren dissect a classroom rat
until Atonement dies before our pens
like blood under a microscopic lens
and Love, before which once we dared not speak,
becomes a mistranslation from the Greek.

Lord, all your gifts are worthy, and forbid
that fruits of scholarship should be kept hid,
but subtle is the pathway to disaster
when all the scholar's study is his master.
O thou who prayed to keep us from temptation
save us now from our imagination
lest — thinking in our ingenuity
it's *you* who falls beneath *our* scrutiny —
we file and reference till we can recall
only the doctrine, not the All-in-All
and let you Lord (it will not save our necks)
be crucified again, by card index.

SIGNS

By the traffic lights
the Indian grocer
promises FOO   VALUE
while over Piccadilly
the red and white neon
of the Coke sign insists
It's the Real Th g
to Eros' downturned stony face.

People are so casual
you'd almost think
it was a matter of
complete indifference
whether or not
you understood things
they have to say,
things like
  ake the plung
and
I th nk
I ove
yo .

ARITHMETIC

That you and I are one is surely true,
yet just as plainly you and I are two,

and now you say (on looking in your heart)
that you against yourself take your own part

and being both the judge and advocate
this civil strife further divides our state —

a fractioning which scarcely makes us three,
for I can see the selfsame thing in me.

So with a schizophrenic sense I draw
this obvious conclusion: we are four.

Small wonder if in heaven there's consternation
at this quadratic amorous equation —

the Lord above is only One-in-Three,
but both of you is one with both of me.

THE PROFESSOR AT WORK

The professor is painting his gate.
  As the sun warms the ground
  the only slight sounds
are the swishes his brush-strokes create.
It is early, some time before eight.
  While his wife slumbers on
  and unhelped by his son
the professor is painting his gate.

The marking of papers must wait.
  Though the act may inflame
  his detractors, who claim
the department is in quite a state
and the standard to which they translate
  the works of Hugo
  is appallingly low,
the professor is painting his gate.

His writings may well fascinate,
  but the proofs lie unread
  by the side of his bed
and his critics, still insatiate,
merely sharpen their pencils and wait —
  while the world remains vague
  on the *Life of d'Antraigues*
the professor is painting his gate.

What becomes of the culture he taught?
   Now the philistine hordes
   are down-treading the boards
has the battle that so long was fought
now been lost? Has the thing become sport?
   Let his colleagues demur —
   alors, le professeur
est en train de peindre sa porte.

Some have said he may one day be great,
   that his restless *esprit*
   courts a rare destiny,
but for now this appointment with fate
is postponed until some future date,
   while the name that lifts eyebrows
   on many French highbrows
is quietly painting his gate.

Now he stops, and his back becomes straight.
   He steps back a pace
   and a smile splits his face.
There is nobody near to ovate
but with pleasure quite commensurate
   with achieving the peak
   of *palmes académiques*
the professor has finished his gate.

PHILOSOPHY

In the unweeded garden of the heart
the dog Philosophy goes
and he wonders if this is a foxglove
and he wonders if this is a rose
and he marks out his patch O so carefully
and the stench goes right up his nose
and he buries his bones and he digs them all up
and he wonders why none of them grows

MR GALLUP REPORTS

Now that truth
is a matter of opinion
we took a poll
to find out what we should believe in.

Reincarnation (27 per cent)
has hit a low point,
but it'll be back.

Satan (30 per cent)
is said to be quietly satisfied
but hopes to do worse next time.
In his opinion
it's better the Devil you don't know
as what you don't know can't hurt you, can it?

Heaven (57 per cent)
sure beats the hell out of
Hell (27 per cent),
a triumph of hope
over experience.

Sin (69 per cent)
despite the best efforts
of social work and education
is sorry to be still so obvious
and after all this time so unoriginal,

while God (76 per cent)
tops the poll
and wonders that so many still believe
yet never bother
to let him know.

THE MAN WHO GOT ON AT EALING

The man
    who got on at Ealing talks
        to strangers. He says

Meaning is
    a function of a discourse situation.
        The leg of his spectacles

is held in place with Sellotape.
    He knew a mathematician called
        Reifenberg, or was it

Reisenberg? The name
    was lost in the tunnel's
        din; in any case

he's dead now, poor chap,
    fell off a mountain in the Dolomites,
        but he could drop his prejudices

instantly, like the man who got on at Ealing
    seeking a mathematical foundation
        for language, his manuscript

sitting in a stranger's lap,
    about to drop a
        bombshell on an unsuspecting world

before the man
    who got on at Ealing Broadway
        gets off.

SQUIGGLES

Maybe God's at home in heaven today.
The sun seems to smile down,
doling out warmth and light
as if just for us.

But we know better.
The sun
is quite indifferent to our welfare
and wouldn't be the least concerned
if Ealing were under permafrost,
or reduced to a small glowing cinder
following a neutron attack
by nine-foot aliens from the planet Zog.

The sun
has quite enough problems of its own,
such as dealing with spots
like any other adolescent star,
and wondering how to get itself a tan.

Yet long ago,
when the human race was in its early laps,
things seemed to be heaven sent.
Sun was a god
riding his chariot across the sky.
Thunder and lightning kept us on our toes.
Stars knew their place.
The moon was lit conveniently most nights.

Then science got down to it —
a private eye digging for dirt,
to prove that his client
had been seriously deceived.

And now
after extensive research
in the features section of *The Guardian*
and the first eight pages of
A Brief History of Time
I can reveal the origins of life itself,
which is to do with
squiggles.

What happened was
15 billion years ago
something went bang
(or maybe more of a whump,
we're still working on that bit)

and the squiggles set off
across whatever was there at the time
to begin the becoming
or become the beginning.

The squiggles spread
and all things being equal would have turned
into a kind of cosmic goo
like Chinese restaurant chicken & sweetcorn soup
without the sweetcorn.

But there were little ripples
like noodles in the soup
which pulled the squiggles
into lumps
and then turned into bits
of things.

Waiter
there's a squiggle in my soup.
Never mind sir
just leave it there long enough
it'll evolve into a fly —
but only if conditions
are favourable.

The other planets didn't have what it takes.
Mercury flew close to the sun
but forgot to revolve
and so it roasts itself on one side
like an abandoned beefburger on a barbeque.

Venus
took the leisure centre approach
but someone must have left the sauna on
for a few billennia

and conditions on Jupiter
have clearly depressed
the market for timeshares,

but evolution,
like Goldilocks
trying out all the possibilities,
found one place that was just right —

it seems that
of all the planets
in all the solar systems
in all the universe
we had to squiggle into this one.

Of course
we may not be alone.
But if there is life elsewhere
it may not be as we know it.

Perhaps elsewhere a squiggle
became a squoggle
and so people on another planet
have three heads and one foot
and Carry On films are there considered the
highest form of culture.

Meanwhile back on earth the squiggles
became hieroglyphics
then an alphabet
and finally a digital display
on the screen of the ultimate Amstrad
working out its view of life
as a series of mathematical equations.

The gaps in which God might be found
are closed up daily.

The tabloids report he was last seen
clothed in a tatty sentimentality
skulking in the doorway of a West End church
cadging coppers from old ladies.

The Amstrad says
the board of superstition
has been swept clean —
prayers are no more use than touching wood,
demons are now exorcised by drugs,
drought is caused not by divine judgement
but by bad management —
cosmic blame can now be laid squarely at the door
of the Anglian Water Authority

and though horoscopes are still quite interesting
it seems that God didn't make
the little green apples,
rainbows are just a trick of the light,
the Man's no longer in the Moon,
our feelings are just nerves following the brain's
        agenda
and words are only noises that we make.

The program writes itself out
towards the Superlaw,
the single, ultimate equation

and as for other explanations
they are just stories,
and stories can't be true
because they can't be proved

and so our dream is that one day
Winnie-the-Pooh will stump off up the forest
to discover the defective gene
which will account for Eeyore,
the wolf will put Red Riding Hood away for ever
and Father Christmas, Jesus and the fairies
will go to Never-Never Land
where they will find security of tenure
in the Department of Psychology

and we shall read our children bedtime algebra,
softly crooning quantum lullabies
as they drift off into the black hole of sleep.

But in their dreams
the theories unravel —

Darwin had a good shot with evolution,
but if only the fittest survive
what can explain the continuing existence
of Spud-U-Like and Barry Manilow?

The hypothesis
that we live in just one
of an infinite number of universes
is surely nothing more than comfort
for Scottish football fans
that somewhere, sometime
they must have qualified for a semi-final,

and if this is the best
of all possible worlds,
then what is Milton Keynes?

The results have come back from the lab
but they're rather disappointing.
Perhaps there's been some kind of mix-up —

is a photograph really no more than black dots?
Is music just a stream of data?
Is a diamond nothing more
than a seriously depressed piece of carbon,
or a kiss only a comprehensive exchange of germs?
Is metaphor coincidence
and art just fashion,
blood a useful carrier of nutrients,
sweat a consequence of overheating
tears an involuntary chemical reaction
caused frequently by death,
which itself is only the molecules
no longer vibrating?

The equations say
that these words here on this page
are nothing more than squiggles:

it seems we have
some work still to do on all this.
Grant applications are pouring in
for more research into the structure
of truth goodness beauty love and evil,
why Keats didn't just write
Ode On A Grecian Squiggle
or Shakespeare pen
All's Well That Ends In Squiggles.

The mathematicians strain to look
over their shoulder to see
who it might be
who turns the dots back into pictures
and noises into music.

Where can we find him?
After we've taken the universe apart
and looked under every piece
of cold, dark matter
and pronounced him missing
(or at least that he's been in a meeting
for a very long time)

will we hear him
walking in the garden of genetics
in the cool of the universe's day?

Or see him
gazing out at us
from the cold, dark matter of the heart
which is not located by telescopes
or susceptible to chemotherapy?

We may well have been fooled,
like the deconstructionist English student
who took his word-processor to pieces
to find the meaning of the poem he'd just written,

and what then if
the point he's really making
as he writes out his universe in its endless
tantalising, well-designed equations
is just one simple, massive overstatement:

"Look at it —
and none of this is of as much value
as the soul that your technology will never find!

Now will you believe me
when I tell you
just how much you are worth?"

This boy curled up on his father's knee
draws squiggles with a felt-tip pen,
coaxing them into significance.
Upon the paper
they turn into a park, a car, a street

and this girl on her garden swing
makes quantum jumps onto the lawn
grinning in a wholly uncalculated way

and above
the sun seems to smile down,
doling out warmth and light
as if just for us.
Maybe God's at home in heaven today.

FOUR TRUTHS

The poorest truth is logical.
Picks its way through stumbling blocks.
When it meets a paradox
bangs its head against a wall.

The second is poetical.
Steps aside where logic sticks.
Swaps around the building bricks.
Has no plan to it at all.

The third is metaphorical,
the most that we can understand,
snapshots of the promised land.
Jesus chose the parable.

The last truth is the best of all:
purpose yet to be revealed,
paradox to be unsealed.
This will take the curtain call.

APOCALYPSO

In the night while we slept
the bombs fell on Tripoli
and up in the Four Horsemen's stables
the grooms lay awake

wondering if this was another fire drill
or if this was the real thing at last.

THE COMFORT OF THE RAIN

Pentecost Sunday,
June Nineteen-Ninety,

and the world hasn't yet
blown its fatal hole in the ozone layer.

Jesus is further delayed
for reasons not fully stated:

the extra nineteen hundred years
have left us time to study eschatology

and learn the meanings of 'the time is short'
which Paul could not have known. Tonight

across the city in a thousand churches
hands will be raised

to a hundred thousand slightly different Gods,
and voices will call down the Spirit's fire

as they called to Baal on Carmel.
But there is no Elijah, no Simon Peter,

no tongue of flame on the wet branches
in this almost-empty park, only these last few
    children

who swing through arcs of gravity,
who spin on the axis of this roundabout

feeling the pull of nameless forces
and the comfort of the rain.

HEROD'S LAST REQUEST

When Herod came to dinner we
locked up the silver cutlery —
though king of God's own chosen nation
he had a certain reputation.
Quite a few later remarked
on how his chariot was parked:
it didn't really do much harm,
just set off the odd car alarm
(and anyway they never use
wing-mirrors on BMWs).
One thing we were grateful for —
his guards remained outside the door.
They said they didn't mind it snowing
and whiled away the time by throwing
javelins at next door's cat
(the neighbour's curtains twitched at that).
We set an extra place or two
for the Ethiopian eunuchs who
he brought along to taste his food.
I said his timing's very good,
dropping by on Christmas Day;
we were entertaining anyway.
Herod chewed the turkey fat
and chatted about this and that —
the cost of temple services,
the relative advantages
of burnt offerings over frankincense —
we seemed to have his confidence
and in a weak, unguarded minute
(just like me to drop us in it)
I brought up, casually aside,
the subject of infanticide.
Remembering John the Baptist's head
I was concerned at what I'd said

but then we saw, to our surprise,
a twinkle came in Herod's eyes.
"Why, don't you know what brought me here?
Well, then I must make it clear!
I've come to pay my compliments
to fellows with a common sense.
Say, don't you think that we might be
in the same business, you and me?
I kill by violence, you neglect —
and here you've earned my deep respect
for I can only be selective:
your methods are much more effective.
Just let an open sewer stink,
give him no clean water to drink
or basic medical supplies
and see how quickly one child dies!
By careful acts of selfishness
you have created such a mess
you now eliminate about—"
(he took his calculator out)
"—forty thousand every day."
He smiled and put the thing away.
"You can destroy whole continents
simply by indifference.
But though I like what you don't do,
your actions are impressive too.
You take the mineral resource,
the inexpensive labour force,
most of the profits they can earn
and then you leave them in return
Coca-Cola and Big Mac,
debts they never can pay back,
spare change you feel good in giving,
cardboard packaging to live in.

A hundred million children now
sleep on the planet's streets somehow
apprenticed into useful trades
like prostitution, drugs and AIDS —
though I'm both cruel and sadistic
I can't compete with that statistic,
nor with the armaments I know
you've built to keep the status quo.
I just had swords and knives and spears
but after nineteen hundred years
you have such powerful weapons
their cost alone kills millions!
However population climbs
you can destroy it fifty times
and fight it on a dozen fronts
while you don't feed it even once.
That's big league stuff compared to me
who butchers a baby boy (or three).
There's nothing more I need to do —
I'll leave my murdering to you.
A toast is called for now, I think.
This Christmas evening let us drink
to all the damage that's been done
by looking after Number One!"
He raised his glass up to his head —
the wine it held was rich and red —
and looking round from face to face
he said "But we should say a grace!
Give thanks to those in direst need
who starve so we can overfeed
and die to do us sinners good.
We eat their flesh and drink their blood.
Do this, as oft as you remember,
at least once every December."

Then Herod laughed, and drained his wine.
Somehow I couldn't stomach mine,
yet though he smiled, his eyes were grim —
something clearly unsettled him.
"I murdered boys aged two or less,
and this was done under duress.
If you should want to place the blame
then put the Magi in the frame:
if I had not been so deceived
by those wise men, then I believe
much blood would never have been spilled.
I only needed one child killed.
My motive was quite rational:
stability in Israel
depends on keeping sweet somehow
whoever's emperor just now.
This story of a new-born king
could only be unsettling:
he was a danger, patently,
to national security
and threatened also therewithal
my throne, my life, my soul, my all.
So — proving that my word is good —
I went just as I said I would
to worship at his incarnation.
He had my total dedication.
Everything was sacrificed
until I found the baby Christ.
And did you think I'd failed? Oh, no.
Though it took thirty years or so
my people got the brat at last
and strung him up and held him fast
and made quite sure that he was dead.
And there he should have stayed. Instead

something went wrong. I don't know how,
I just know he is not dead now
and like a nightmare in my brain
it happens time and time again —
with lives for stables, hearts for mangers,
he is born to total strangers
and so I cannot rest secure
until the child is found once more
and the botched work of Calvary
is completed finally.
That's why I'm here, and why I stay,
for now a billion times a day
those nails are hammered deeper in
by each act of your human sin
and, though each time the God-man dies
somehow he manages to rise,
still there may be — I don't despair —
evil enough to hold him there.
If Christ is born again in you
is he not often murdered too?
Surely someone hates enough
to overcome this power of love?
I depend on you, you see.
Please, finish off this job for me."

CONVERT

He came to
faith in
All Souls,
but it wasn't
until much later
that finally
he came to
faith in
all circumstances.

DISCIPLE

I will follow you.

I will go the the ends of the earth for you
    so long as the earth is round.

I will die to the flesh
    in the sure and certain hope of resurrection.

I will put away the old man
    for safe keeping.

Your yoke is easy —
    that's good.
I don't mind what it costs
    if I can afford it.

I don't mind doing my bit on the cross.
    We could have a rota.
    Put me down for a couple of hours
    Sunday evening

    and please don't use nails.

I will follow you
    carefully,
    with helpful advice.

I will follow you
    wherever I want to go.

PEACE

We may say "It is peaceful",
but this is not peace.
This is just the absence of noise.
Somewhere noise goes on —
in the ambulance sirens,
in the sweat-shops in Hong Kong,
in the veins of the addict,
in the minds of the wrongly-imprisoned
and the mother of the cot-death baby
the noise goes on but we don't hear it.
Our ears are plugged
with the wax of self-importance
so we say "It is peaceful",
but it is not God's peace.
This is the peace the world gives
and its real name is pride.

We may say "We live at peace",
but this is not peace.
This is just the absence of war.
Somewhere war goes on —
in parts of America,
through half of Asia,
across most of Africa,
in the shopping centres of Ulster
and the litter bins of London
the war goes on but we don't see it.
We have turned our eyes away
because it won't happen here,
so we say "We live at peace",
but it is not God's peace.
This is the peace the world gives
and its real name is indifference.

We may say "Now, he is at peace"
but this is not peace.
This is just the absence of life.
Somewhere life goes on —
in the house he never owned,
in the job he almost finished,
in the children he meant to talk to,
in the wife he failed to love,
in the father he couldn't remember
and the mother he wouldn't forgive
life goes on but he doesn't live it,
so we say "Now, he is at peace",
but it is not God's peace.
This is the peace the world gives
and its real name is death.

The peace of God
is nothing like this.
It is more like noise.
It is more like war.
It is more like life.

The peace of God
is like the peace of the tightrope walker
balancing a hundred feet above Niagara Falls.

It is in the peace of the cancer patient
for whom treatment is no longer prescribed.

It is in the peace
in the quiet moment
after the fatal road accident.

It is in the peace
of a ruined, liberated city.

It is in the peace
at the centre of the whirlwind
that tears the island to pieces.

It is in the peace
at the opening of the gates
of Auschwitz.

It is the peace of the man
who has lost everything
so has nothing else to lose.

It is the peace of Stephen
as the first stones
bruise his body.

It is the peace of Gethsemane, saying
Nevertheless your will be done.

It is the peace of the carpenter
as he steadies his hammer
for the last blow on the nail.

It is the peace of the women
on their necessary business
in the desolate dawn.

AT GRASMERE

The blue-
black mayfly danced
for half a minute
by my shoe.

Tessa was glad.
"How sad
to live for a day
if nobody knew".

DRUNKARD

When first it was offered
a drop was enough —
you weren't even sure
that you liked the stuff,

but you were quite young
and your palate was chaste —
with some perseverance
you soon got the taste.

You could take it or leave it?
That's what they all think.
Soon your only desire
was for just one more drink.

Now it's straight from the bottle,
not even a cup,
and you splutter and hiccup
and bring it back up

and bloated and bleary
you lurch into bed,
not one ounce of remorse
in your stupefied head.

Well you're satisfied now
but you don't know till when,
and first thing in the morning
you're at it again —

it's not whisky or gin
(who on earth would drink *that*!)
it's the thin white warm hard stuff
that lays you out flat

you may sleep through the night
and you don't suffer colic
but, baby, you know
you're a real milkaholic.

NAPPY CHRISTMAS

Awash in a manger
the baby awakes

we didn't buy Peaudouce
we all make mistakes

THE HOUSEWIFE'S EVENING PRAYER

I hope I'll go to heaven
but I'd like to know one thing:
in the Father's many mansions
who does the hoovering?

I'd love to join the feasting
and drink the bridegroom's cup,
but could you reassure me
about the washing up?

Are the angels' haloes polished?
Do their tunics fit alright?
And do any little cherubs
need a bottle in the night?

Of course I'm sure that everything
we do there will be nice,
but absolutely nothing
would make it paradise.

POEM FOR CHRISTMAS EVE

This is a love story, if you can accept it,
that God the father looked down at his world
and the world was like a sleeping, fitful child
and the child was spoiled.

Its nations called each other names
and roamed earth's playground like a gang of boys
who choose sides, always brandishing
their terrifying toys.

The world thought it was fatherless and hunted
restlessly for some new sign or token —
as if Christmas had come and gone, its presents all
unwrapped, already broken,

and the father God looked at his child and counted
the cost of love's freedom: but he had a plan,
to step from out of time and into history
and become a man.

With eternity to find the spot he chose
with the greatest care. One night a workman stood
in a barn with a group of animals
watching the birth of God

while out on the hills some shepherds were
    astonished
as a skyful of angels appeared then disappeared,
and a few astrologers saw a change in the stars
they'd studied for years

and almost everyone else knew nothing.
Caesar turned and settled in his luxurious bed
while in Bethlehem the power and the glory
bawled for milk in a shed.

It was quite an entrance. The only Son of God
homeless, illegitimate, a refugee,
owning nothing but the world that he grew up in
had made himself quite empty,

his birth itself a kind of dying where
he abdicated power, omniscience,
was needy, hated and misunderstood
and after the last violence

he was laid in the womb of a grave for the birth
which Bethlehem merely anticipated
and for which the blind, brave, barricaded
spoiled world waited —

no sage or rustic came with gifts,
only some women, hopelessly brave,
brought spices in the dark of morning
to an empty grave.

Two deaths, two births, the manger and the cross:
the first brought hope, the second brought salvation.
Out of his poverty this child has made us rich
beyond imagination,

and on a winter evening in a London home
a father looks down at his sleeping child.
The room is warm and brightly lit. Outside
the night is darkly wild,

and the child that sleeps knows well that she is
    loved,
and in her bones knows how to disobey,
and she will learn that none is innocent,
that death takes all away,

and the father looking at her peaceful face
feels his own helplessness and counts the cost
of the love between them in a spoiled world
where all must end in loss

but for Bethlehem and Calvary. These births
have brought an end to death,
and the child in the manger is the Lord
we feed on in our hearts by faith

now and forever. Child, if you would wake
on this Christmas Eve outside you'd find
a star, not a streetlamp. Listen, you can hear
the angels' message in the wind.

MONSTER

We don't know the planet
the monster came from, only that

it is here now and cannot return.
The keepers are not sure if it is harmful.

It is like a chameleon or a spaceman
(it has pointed ears — perhaps it was on Star Trek).

They prod it to make sure it's still alive.
The monster stirs. Its face

is nearly recognisable. The keepers feed it
as much as they are able, and sometimes

the monster seems to humour them until
they almost think it may be tamed — but then

the monster roars and will not be consoled.
The keepers watch it, knowing now

they cannot penetrate its private grief,
and fear the wordless rage that tortures it. At night

it is kept behind bars for its own protection.
They try to make it comfortable.

The monster smiles. The keepers both relax,
rocking it into a milky sleep.

Told You So

Obedient to the latest thinking
of the Sunday Times medical experts
we raise the head of Emma's cot
two inches off the ground
with *The Pelican Guide*
to English Literature
under one leg
balanced up with
Keats' Collected Works.

Now I sleep doubly secure
knowing my daughter
will safely breathe,
and reassured in my belief
that poetry can make
the difference
between life
and death
after all.

VOCATION

Others built cities,
crossed continents
and changed history.

He built sentences,
crossed t's
and changed typefaces.

He said God
why did it have to be words?
And God said

In the beginning
consider the cost
of my silence.

BEIRUT

When all this trouble started
I wrote a poem about you, Beirut.
It took me a very long time.
It was done with the utmost sensitivity.

You weren't grateful.
Politicians on all sides denounced it.
Militias ignored it.
Despite the support of many Western governments
the poem never had a chance.
Olive-skinned fanatics
with immaculate moustaches
told American newscasts
they would never recognise the poem
and all the time
plotted its annihilation.

When I finally got through to the poem
I could hardly recognise it myself.
Not a stanza was intact.
Shelling had been especially heavy
around the adjectives.
The bloody words just lay there
pleading for their pathetic lives.

It was over in seconds.
I hit the wastebin
rat a tat tat
without a ricochet.

BEN FRANKLIN

When
in 1751
Ben Franklin
found out how lightning worked

cathedrals everywhere
put up conductors
to deflect thunderbolts
from heaven.

Another weapon gone
in the fight against heresy
sighed God,
changing tactics yet again.

THE DEVIL'S TINDER BOX

He killed people. He was no more
than a boy flying in a box with wings.

Four times down went the box, each time
with another crew up and so

he missed becoming a statistic and survived
to spend his life working statistics out.

The simple honesty which later marked
his handling of business affairs

would have been with him then: he must have killed
reluctantly but well. I only heard him talk

once about his thirteenth mission, on
February Thirteenth — he said

if ever his number was up
that should have been it; but by 1945

even daylight raids were almost unopposed —
with the Luftwaffe beaten they bombed more or less
    at will.

The dilemma that he faced was exquisite:
to do his job well, as he knew he must,

meant killing ever more effectively
those who were neither enemies nor friends,

whose weakness robbed the fliers of all excuses
but that they followed orders (the defence

that wouldn't serve at Nuremburg). On the
night of the Devil's Tinder Box

they knew what they were doing. The target,
all but unguarded, had no strategic value

but its railway, and was swelled with refugees
from Stalin's push west. *Poor bastards*, he said

all those years later, in a voice
I had never heard before. With the war already won

Dresden was still beautiful as my father
settled in the belly of the plane,

a wheel-hub (all bomb-aimers did this) shielding
his private parts from the chance caress

of a lucky shell from the untrained
flak guns of the terrified men below.

They Had No Credit Cards

They had no credit cards said the manager
They could have been anyone

Sheep must be protected said the bishop
They're so easily upset

It's a vicious little province said the governor
You can't make allowances

How could we have known who it was
Tell us how we could have known

Because it's always me said the dead man
Tricky isn't it, it's always me.

BODY ODOUR

This man whose arms are raised in prayer
exalts his Lord above the skies.
The Spirit rules him while he's here.
His wife controls him otherwise.

This woman prays with feeling for
the missionaries in Peru
while managing to quite ignore
the others sitting in the pew,

and this man, when the ritual's done,
wonders why it is that those
who are the fragrance of the Son
so often just get up his nose.

He lets all kinds of people in.
Here is your mother, sister, brother.
We eat and drink the stuff of sin.
This is the church. There is no other.

A LAODICEAN ESTATE AGENT WRITES

The developers have moved in
on 1 Corinthians 13
(a delightful period chapter
retaining many of its original features)

The structural survey found
Faith, Hope and Love
inadequate for modern requirements

The valuers found
that it profited them nothing

The planning office saw
as in a glass, darkly

The architect
believed all things

The contractor
hoped all things

The neighbours
endured all things

The builders
spoke with tongues of men
and definitely not angels

and now it's done and back on the market
these three remain
Ambition, Fear and Need

and the greatest of these
is never satisfied

You Can't Be Too Careful

The old lady
in the pew behind
exchanged the peace with me

but went up for Communion
clutching her handbag
just in case

Notes for a Biography

When Jesus went to Bethlehem
I must say it was odd
I wouldn't have been born that way
if I was being God

When Jesus went to Nazareth
he spent twenty years in trade
that's hardly a career
in which Messiahs will be made

When Jesus picked his followers
a practised eye could tell
he was plainly inexperienced
at hiring personnel

When Jesus wandered Palestine
it was awfully hit and miss
you'll never reach your customers
with marketing like this

When Jesus worked a miracle
you don't need a degree
to know that healing on the sabbath
will annoy a Pharisee

When he went to Jerusalem
he rode there on an ass
what a PR opportunity
and Jesus let it pass

When he went to Gethsemane
the game was not yet up
there was time for him and Judas
to kiss and make it up

When Jesus stood in Pilate's house
he didn't realise
that politics is all about
the art of compromise

When Jesus went to Calvary
that's the ending of the story
one more tragic hero
death instead of glory

He must have been mad
that's the only way I understand it
when Jesus went to Calvary
you'd almost think he'd planned it

DREAM

Woke before the alarm. Pulled
the covers over my head
but you can't avoid the day for ever. Outside
the windscreen was white with frost. Poured
a kettleful of water over it and drove
squinting through the frozen rivulets.
         One theory is
dreams are the way that the unconscious mind
sorts the day's debris, like a berserk computer —
fear, loss, guilt, desire, the girl in the mirror
at the traffic lights, in dark glasses . . . how is it
I never dream about you, God?

ABERDARON

We may suppose he has been here. There is
evidence, this bay, this headland,

the clouds' endless commentary
as if to say *See what was done*

with one word, and so many millennia
We must suppose it. Nothing

else will free the hung jury of our reason,
like a child in a game

counting to ten, to a hundred, a thousand —
Ready or not, here I come! Silence

and the shadow of a gull's wing on the water,
the slow breaking of the sea.

THE WORD'S OUT

Sometimes
I listen for your word
and hear nothing.

In the quiet of my room
the only noise
is the thump of my own heart
and angry voices arguing in my head.

You can't say I don't give you a chance.
Sometimes I may say nothing
for as long as five minutes.
Your silence is still deafening.

But then I open a book
and out tumbles your voice.
And when I try to shut that up
I find you can get a word in anywhere.

I've even heard you sometimes from the pulpit.

I hear you on the Nine O'Clock News
saying "What have you done
with the world I gave you?"

I hear you in the tabloids
saying "Whoever is without sin
cast the first stone."

With the first burst of spring flowers
you say "Look — no hands!"

With the most extraordinary sunset
you say "Look, just relax".

The shrunken face of hunger
is you saying "Feed me".

The beggar on the underground
is you saying "House me".

The dreaded diagnosis
is you saying "Heal me".

The valium prescription
is you saying "Free me".

The redundancy notice
is you saying "Value me".

The scream of the torture victim
is you saying "Father, forgive".

The priest staring down the barrel of a gun
is you saying "Love casts out fear".

When I am late and hurrying
you are the face on the clock
saying "I am the beginning and the end".

When I am greedy
you are the face on the banknote
saying "Treasure is in heaven".

When I am proud
you drop your banana-skins in front of me
saying "Don't look down".

When I am lonely
you are the stillness of the house
saying "I am with you, always".

And when I am grieving
you are the voice at the graveside
saying "I am the Resurrection and the Life".

Sometimes
I listen for your word
and hear nothing.

And sometimes
you make so much noise
I can hardly hear anything else.

HOME IMPROVEMENTS

You can't trust anyone these days.
Take this Jesus.
Seemed OK.
We asked him in,
just being neighbourly, the way you do.

Over dinner he was pleasant enough
apart from an annoying habit
of turning the small talk into conversation.
Even seemed keen to hear about
our plans for home improvements.
So we showed him round.

This was the big mistake.
When it came down to it
he wasn't really interested
in the kitchen units
or the bathroom tiles
or the artificial ceiling in the lounge,
but kept peering into cupboards uninvited
(as if we had dry rot)
and prizing up the edges of the carpet
(as if we had woodworm)

and finally disappeared into the cellar
(heaven knows what he found down there)
emerging with a hammer
and a pickaxe
and a drill
and a pocketful of drawings
and smiling in a most alarming way said
I've just had a much better idea

and started smashing down the walls

VISITOR

What is that rushing sound
where all has been so quiet?
Who howls around this house
making the blood run riot?

Who is it that he seeks?
What passion in him strains
that he should shake the doors
and crack the window panes?

What comfort will he bring
or anguish bring about?
What if we let him in?
We cannot keep him out —

it is the breath of God:
at Pentecost he came
there to embrace his love
in arms of leaping flame,

a cold and silent fire
that burns within the soul
until it is consumed
into the purest gold.

PHANTOM

The limb removed, the amputee
swears there's an itching where
hand or foot was,
a ghostly memory
of something once attached.

There are phantom people too.
It's unimportant, almost
nothing, just some trick
on eye and mind
of a slight, familiar imprint —

a motorway sign, a certain
tilt of a woman's head.

Runner

'We don't have a climate, only weather',
and plenty of it. Tessa

hates it, it keeps her inside. I put on
my rain-suit with the hood drawn tight and splash

seven or eight miles along the river,
my Nikes soaked through and half the Thames
    Basin

to wash off in the bathtub when I get back home.
You need to run on days like these

when the wind gusts force nine up the river
throwing the past at you in bucketsful

and even memory loses its nerve.
You need to outrun the ghosts

that crowd the river path under the trees
and brush like nettles as you race past,

these faces, hostages of the storm,
lovers and those who were never lovers

and someone once, a girl, a woman really,
I don't say I knew her well — these dreams

that are lies, such lies
they are better left in the rain on the darkening path

as I stand panting for breath outside my own front
    door.
I love my wife. My study is a tidy room

full of questions stacked on bricks and planks —
Knowing God, Sex in the Real World,

How to Manage Pressure, Running to Win —
which will stay unanswered for another six months

at which time the whole lot comes down
to make way for a cot and a baby,

and I will sit then
in the room at the back of the house

hearing this weather above my typewriter's clatter,
hearing the rainfall at the end of summer, drumming

on garden leaves in the cool of the evening
the endless whisper, *Love me more than these.*

THE FLYING PROFESSOR

When they're stacking for miles above Orly
and Heathrow is shrouded in fog
and the captain of many a grounded plane
makes an entry of gloom in his log,

when the seat reservation computer
has crashed and gone down with all hands
and the bags have been sent to Vancouver
when the labels said Grange-over-Sands,

to a seasoned air traffic controller
the reason is perfectly plain,
and the crews all exchange knowing glances —
  the professor is flying again.

In the queue at gate B27
in Melbourne or Bangkok or Rome
he is clutching his boarding card tightly
like the key to his second home,

and the faces all seem so familiar
as he settles down into his seat,
and they hand him the *Herald Tribune*
and they hand him a purple boiled sweet

and the widebodied 747
taxis off with immaculate care
till it charges headfirst down the runway
and climbs up to heaven knows where.

While he's the first to acknowledge
that travel has broadened his mind
he suspects it of having an equal effect
on his waistline and on his behind,

so he presses the recline button
and kicks off his travelling shoes
and pulling the eyeshade down over his face
drifts off into sleep — well, a snooze —

and he's snug in his blow-up neck collar
with the plugs nestled tight in his ear
and the stewardess straightens his blanket
and whispers "Rest now, you poor dear . . ."

In the legends of aviation
a tragic new tale has begun,
as poignant as Icarus seeking
a weekend away in the sun —

it's the curse of the Flying Professor
condemned to stay up in the air
because half of his family lives over here
while the other half lives over there.

And sometimes, when changing at Frankfurt
or stopping for fuel in Bahrein,
his future life passes before him
in the form of a journey by plane.

Like a scene from a play by Sam Beckett
he is somewhere that's just in between,
writing pieces on shopping in Aix-la-Chapelle
for Aer Lingus in-flight magazine.

He can't find the summoning button
as the stewardess flashes a smile,
and he's one seat away from the window
and he's one seat away from the aisle

tied up in an orange lifejacket
that will never completely inflate
while another light meal is served every half hour
and left, just out of reach, on a plate.

They hit little pockets of turbulence,
as you do on the smoothest of trips,
which come at precisely the moment
he lifts his full cup to his lips.

The film is something from New Zealand
that has not reached the cinemas yet
and he can't seem to alter his earphones
which are tuned in to Tammy Wynette

and he quietly fingers his sick-bag
for he's not one for making a fuss
but perhaps it's the slight whiff of sulphur
that's making him so nauseous —

and he has an uneasy feeling
as the FASTEN YOUR SEATBELT sign warns
he could swear that the grinning attendant
was wearing a small pair of horns —

as the tyre-rubber burns on the runway
he knows there's as much of a chance
of his reaching the end of these wanderings
as Glenn Miller of landing in France,

and he's sure now he journeys in vain to escape
the conclusion he cannot resist:
if it's better to travel in hope than arrive
he's the world's number one optimist.

CARRICK

In case Galilee proved a disappointment
this was the understudy,

the hillsides green and suitable for preaching,
the fishing good, sudden squalls

giving way to miraculous calms,
weather that, like Him, each day decides

whether to be wind or fiery sun,
earth tremor or the still and quiet voice.

FIRST LESSON

Peter at the cock-crow
Jonah in his fish

before you get the glory
it always comes to this

THE ECONOMICS OF CALVARY

Here
is the only successful
planned free-market
in the history of the world,

where the cost of living
and the wages of sin
are the same

and the rate of exchange is fixed
at one life
given as a ransom
for many.

Has Anybody Here Seen Thomas?

Sometimes I feel
like an Easter Saturday,
                            just
a tombful of possibilities
wishing my guard
would fall asleep.

MARY

And if you ask me what a Christian is
I'd say, not him who's pure in word and deed,
or goes to all the Sunday services,
or says his prayers, or knows the proper creed,

but that one who would gladly give away
all that he has now or has ever been
to stand between the dark tomb and the day
and know the moment of the Magdalene.

BREAKING THE CHAINS

My first escape bid
came at the age of nought.
Nine months in mummy's tummy —
no more room in the womb.
So with the help of nothing
but two midwives,
one anxious father
and the best technology the NHS had to offer
(I've always been a gambler)
I made my dash for freedom,
lowering myself carefully
on the umbilical cord
ready for the big push.

I got caught.
They threw me in the crib
for six months solitary confinement,
then two years in the cot and playpen
with nappies off for good behaviour.

With native cunning I survived
playschool and nursery,
but from then on
it was just one institution after another
until at eighteen
I came out from behind bars
and began leaning on them instead.

It soon became clear
my family was keeping me under house arrest.
My children
were born in captivity,

and then one day with a shock I found
I had been taken hostage.
I was held alone
in a small room
for seven to eight hours at a stretch
with the minimum of comfort —
a bare desk,
a swivel chair,
a secretary,
two telephones,
an American Express card
and five weeks holiday a year.

At weekends I got parole.
I began to look everywhere
for some hope of freedom.

I combed the Sunday papers
and collapsed exhausted under the weight
of the supplements.

I bought a microwave
a dishwasher
and many labour-saving devices
but they just left me in a vacuum.

I asked my bank manager
who said he could find no interest
in anything free.

I reached for it
in a love affair with no strings
and still got tangled up
when I pulled the other one.

Looking deep into my personal computer
I typed ESCAPE?
and it replied
UNSPECIFIED COMMAND OR FILENAME

I searched for it on a desert island
with only eight gramophone records
and Sue Lawley for company
but I got fed up being asked questions
so I got away
on a raft of unused Bibles left by previous castaways.

I opened negotiations with the Devil
who couldn't promise freedom as such
but offered some interesting terms.

By now I had worked out
where everyone else had gone wrong
in the past.
They had made the mistake
of dying,
so I trained my body and mind
not to be a slave to anything.

I nearly made it.
If I could just have controlled
a few small details

like my temper,
my sex drive,
my need to eat and drink
and my annoying habit of falling unconscious
for eight hours every day,
I'm sure I would have found freedom.

Finally I set out to look for it on the open road
in my XR3i GT soft-top Cabriolet
nought to sixty in 4.5 seconds
but I got stuck in traffic
in the Wandsworth one-way system,

so I dialled it up on my car phone
and I got its answering machine
I'M SORRY FREEDOM IS
NOT AVAILABLE AT THE MOMENT
PLEASE LEAVE A MESSAGE
AFTER THE ATONEMENT

I had run out of ideas.
Turning on my radio I realised
I was not alone.
Whole countries were trying to get out.
Eastern Europe had made a break for it
leaving the Iron Curtain on the latch
and just a few short range missiles for cover.

The USA
had built itself a space shuttle
but it only took six people at a time
and anyway it kept coming back.

The Soviet Union
in desperation
attempted to declare
independence from itself,

while Britain
just tried to tunnel its way out.

Nobody made it.
It was easy to be wise after the event —
with all that pent-up anger,
banged up in the world day after day,
slopping out into the seas and oceans,
living three or four to a house in intolerable
        conditions
with nothing to do all day but live and die
it just had to e x p l o d e

They rioted in the squares,
they lit fires in the rainforests,
they made holes in the roof.

It was as if they'd found out
that the prison was inside them
and they were held by chains
of pride and fear and death,

they were guilty but were hoping
that there might be some helpful miscarriage of
        justice,
and they were looking for a fresh alibi
when God came innocently by
disguised as a man
saying If the Son shall make you free
you shall be free

and they said Indeed
We don't like your kind coming in here
You're not a normal offender
You interfere with people

Take that they said
handing him a crown
And that they said
look we've had a little whip round for you

and they said
anything you say will be taken down
and used against you
and God said nothing
and it was taken down
and used against him

and here they said
is something we're really cross about.
It's our little way of saying
we blame our parents
we blame society
we blame somebody else
we blame you.
Here is your fixed penalty,
fixed to this wooden beam.

But they didn't know
that each nail they hammered
through his wrists and ankles
broke a link of the chain that bound them

and when he said
It is finished
and they shut him up
under maximum security
tightly wrapped
behind a stone
behind a seal
behind a guard
and dead
just to be on the safe side

after a little while
they heard him say
Here I am
I've found the way out
and come back for you

all charges against you have been dropped
you're free to go
and follow me

or else stay here
in the prison of yourself
if you're afraid of what it might be like
on the outside

the chains are broken,
look, it's you who's holding them together.

TEDDY BEARS

When we have set all this aside —
name, reputation, history —
it will not be for us to slide
into dull uniformity.

Heaven will not level down.
These things that we identify
as most emphatically our own
have less to do with you and me

than we can here imagine.
They stand to life as a cartoon,
mere toys of personality.
We shall forget them quite as soon

as a small child who suddenly
puts aside his teddy bears
and runs, quite unselfconsciously,
to greet his Father on the stairs.

THE SAILING OF THE ARK

INTRODUCTION

The Sailing of the Ark is a sequence of forty-five poems written over a period of four years from December 1987. It was given its first public reading in Ealing in December 1991.

In the early 1980s, having accepted that Jesus Christ is God incarnate, I gratefully embraced the security of the contemporary evangelical pattern of thinking. But it now seems to me (and, I have since found, to others) that it is simply unable to cope with the paradoxes that everywhere lie beneath its fragile surface. It was a creed spelled out in black and white certainties, and the God of the wilderness and the manger was not to be pinned down so easily.

This is not an attack or a rejection: it is simply a moving on. I would have liked all the evangelical myths to have been true; but the Ark insisted on sailing. Nor is it a negative poem. It is about a mystery, and mystery is at the heart of faith. Dogma can be as hard a chain to break as sin.

The sequence is in the form of a letter to a friend, and I am very grateful to Andrew for agreeing to let it be published unchanged.

The drawing of a crucifixion on page 151 is based on sketches for a wood and steel sculpture by Scilla Verney, made shortly before her death from cancer. It is reproduced with the kind permission of her husband Stephen.

The style — a loose form of sonnet without rhyme or strict metre — was borrowed from the late New Zealand poet, James K Baxter.

The poem contains a number of quotations and references, biblical and otherwise. There is not space enough to acknowledge them all here, but should any reader feel it is worth the trouble a set of notes to the sonnets is available from Wordsout (free, but please send sae).

GR

THE SAILING OF THE ARK

To A.C.

We that are bound by vows, and by Promotion,
With pomp of holy Sacrifice and rites,
To teach belief in good and still devotion,
To preach of Heaven's wonders and delights:
Yet when each of us in his own heart looks
He finds the God there far unlike his Books.

Fulke Greville "Chorus Of Priests"

As the heavens are higher than the earth,
so are my ways higher than your ways
and my thoughts than your thoughts.

Isaiah 55:9

1

Andrew, another year has stripped
the leaves, like misconceptions, from the trees;

the last page of the kitchen calendar
prepares to drop, announcing the advent

of that season when, according to good scholarship,
Jesus couldn't have been born. The resurrection

waits on the other side of winter, and in
this month that asks for no apologies

the winds of daily living have laid bare
the root and branches of our faith — what

is it that remains when it has shed
all that's deciduous, its stark wooden

outline raised against the backdrop of this grey,
late-century, turbulent post-Christian sky?

2

Well, Andrew, we've reached life's middle ground,
surprised we got this far without being

found out, and still wondering
what it is we're going to do when we grow up; yet

I'm here somehow with all the regular stuff —
job, wife, mortgage, bank statements and bills,

bathroom ceiling needing papering,
two children to be got to bed by eight — while

the man I might have been digs with his bare hands
in the ruins of a bombed-out house in Basra

or lies on the ground in Africa with ribs
like a birdcage stretched across with parchment

and staring eyes fixed, I think, on something other
than a choice of curtains and the current mortgage
    rate.

3

Balding, overweight, at night I plod
the roads of W5 and W13,

a three-mile token gesture of a run,
dreaming of perfect mortal fitness,

dreaming that round the edge of Walpole Park
I shall one day run and not grow weary.

Jesus kept fit by walking, I suppose —
he never had a desk job, or grew old. I can recall

the day you left All Souls I met your father,
slow and wrinkled, as became his age —

yet once I heard the wireless commentary
on the 1936 Olympic Final

with your dad leading for six hundred metres
then fading, Lovelock coming through to win.

4

It's a numbers game. Our worth is measured out
on sets of calibrated scales. I'm 38,

drive a 2.2 GLE with heated seats
and ran a marathon in 2 hours 49. They give me

umpty tumpty thousand pounds a year
for naming things and organising them,

formulating Numbers for the Beast.
Apocalyptic? No, you've seen the codes,

those neat black beast-marks, such an efficient
    system,
across our cereal packs, even in our Bibles —

God knows, Andrew, I'm helping to promote them!
What nonsense! Why, we even got his birthday
    wrong —

Christ who was born in 4 or 5 BC
laughs and weeps at us, his self-made ciphers.

5

At thirty-five thousand feet,
wearied of business, I looked out to see

the winter sun throw into sharp relief
a barren land of mountains, a fine show

of geology's inhumanity to man.
A drift of cloud had settled on Geneva

like a quilt thrown on a bed — what light or warmth
has the tiny match-flame of our creativity

against all this? Of course he made it,
just as he made the cold terrain of the psyche

or soul, or spirit, call it what you will,
with its unclimbed ridges and deeper valleys,

and some always in shadow, however high
the sun of righteousness rises on healing wings.

6

Some of our friends who came so earnestly
to those lectures and courses, they live now

with things we thought untenable — divorced,
or practising homosexuality, or they just gave it up,

finding that model of the Christian life
came to pieces in their hands, their hard-earned
    knowledge

icing failure with guilt. Was it sin?
Or faithlessness? Or was there also

a lack of power in that theology, tried
and exhausted by experience, its careful

applications weak appeasement to the deep
imperatives of our disordered minds and bodies,
    waved

like Chamberlain's fluttering paper —"Peace in our
    time"—
against the darker annexations of the human will?

7

The wind roared unannounced across
the reclaimed islands of the Ganges delta,

dumping enough ocean to wash away
a hundred thousand lives, most of them children,

and a million homes besides. The sea
returns in time the mercifully drowned:

those who remain are those who must endure
the loving care of God. If your daughter asked for
    bread

would you give her a stone? Then how much more
will be the anguish of the father

in the eyes of his dying child
for whom he can do nothing? If the poor

are so blessed, Andrew, thank God he does not often
    send
beatitudes as wonderful as this.

8

The siren voices of false certainty
re-phrase with seamless arguments

the serpent's many-layered lie
to each succeeding generation: Goebbels,

Saatchi and the host of cults and gurus
prove and re-prove the prophet's words —

"a man hears what he wants to hear
and disregards the rest." The last

tragedy in Eden was not the fall
from innocence, but the deal itself:

the fruit was rotten. The knowledge
for which Adam sacrificed his all turned out to be

no more than gullibility — having swallowed the
    apple
it seems we'll swallow almost anything.

9

So much that at one time seems unassailable
flickers and fades like a dream. We were conceived

in the womb of relative ignorance, inheritors
of certain sets of workable hypotheses —

a shopping-trolley loaded with beliefs —
and in the trials of circumstance our faith

or its nonentity is shaped from what happens to us,
or driven by it flat into the ground. The

lightning flashes of experience
illuminate the chasm that divides

our creed from what we actually believe —
orthodoxy and atheism are alike,

tents where a refugee faith camps
out of the unrelenting weather of the harder
      questions.

10

You're writing about marriage — there's a double
    irony
I know you'll smile at! You, the one-time model
    bachelor! But then

that it should be the issue that broke
you from your first church — that's a tougher one.

Of course the dogma puts half America
into spiritual no-man's land — *Shouldn't*'s a poor
    sermon

for those who've vowed and failed, and try again;
in the bed they've made (if you'll forgive the
    metaphor)

they have to find some way to lie. Whatever you
    write, Andrew,
I hope there'll be comfort "for our hardness of
    heart".

There's no Eden to go back to. The apple
has been eaten, from its thrown core

those trees have grown on whose fruit we have to
    live,
our only *Sitz im Leben* is in their shade.

11

The world is spoiled and cannot be redeemed
piecemeal by liberal or green do-goodery.
   Graphs

grow exponentially, earth
performs its great strip-tease, and for a finale

will disappear up its own backside
with quite astonishing ease, to the applause

of constant economic growth. False Christs
queue at McDonalds; the elect

wander in the myths of Sunday colour magazines
reading of earthquakes and rumours of wars

in which the disarmed ideologies embrace
beneath the icons of material prosperity — this
   abomination

that brings desolation, this god of matter
to whose altar we have been dragged smiling to be
   sacrificed.

12

What little I know of scientific method
tells me a theory is no use that only fits

ninety-five per cent of the results —
it's in the other five that truth lies, Andrew,

on the margins of experience
our gospel is defined. In the Gadarene tombs

Christ and the madman have finished their business
and while we, clothed and in our right minds

consider what it means for us here and now
he has given us the slip, crossing

the dark, storm-bothered waters of Gennesaret
to 42nd Street and Auschwitz: the pimps, drunks,
    addicts,

psychotics, murderers and those whom they
    destroy,
these will be redeemed, or nobody at all.

13

The ark sailed sometime in the 1980s.
The animals went in two by two

or seven by seven depending on which source takes
    precedence:
its motley cargo — Jonah's fish, Job's friends,

ten-foot Goliath, Balaam's talking ass,
limping Jacob, branded Cain, the subtil snake, even

the primal pair themselves, naked and
    unashamed —
all herded in with Noah and his sons.

That clear blue evangelical assurance
clouded over with the cumulus

of archaeology and reasoned common sense
in ever-darkening folds; beneath its weight

the heavens bowed. The muddy deluge broke. The
    ark
sailed out of history and into myth.

14

Here, Andrew, is the plain good news — God
died immortal, loves all men equally

and some more equally than others,
comes not to judge but to judge, brings peace

with a sword, frees us
into complete subjection where first

is last, poor rich, and folly wisdom, where at the end
all shall be united, and split up.

One God, three Gods, the riddle of the Trinity;
God-man, the paradox of incarnation;

King of a world ruled by somebody else,
who makes disciples of their own free will — this is

the God whom we believe and don't believe.
And this we call the simple gospel truth.

15

And still there is the old familiar puzzle
how can He be omnipotent and good?

Did he use his power to manufacture evil?
Or have the will, but lack the means to stop it?

Or if, as it must be, neither can be true,
how should we comprehend this suffering God

who kills us with his endless loving-kindness?
    The question has
defeated the best minds that he made: this
    dreadful love

laid out the context for its own rejection, gave
to its beloved the gift of doubt, and mental tools

to fashion arguments to justify it; and then stood
    back,
watching as into the vacuum of its withdrawal

sin rushed like a wind, a kinetic power
as insubstantial as a hurricane.

16

Two hundred million years ago
a diplodocus waded in the swamps

of Hammersmith, its tiny brain
untroubled by thoughts of God, who no doubt
    looked

as lovingly upon him as later
with tenderness he would watch over simple,

savage men at Easter Island or Stonehenge, their
    short lives
broken on the megaliths of their deeply held
    untruths —

for them it was not the *kairos*, the right time,
and no doubt they will be judged by their lights

in the folly of their generations
by this curious, demanding, secret God

who gazes down from somewhere as his universe
expands hopefully to meet him.

17

We must return to sources, to this holy
and wholly extraordinary book into which

we read back our favourite doctrines, sharing
the comfort of the party line, determined

to make life what we think it ought to be
until our faith becomes a form of words — this

is conspiracy, not truth: incarnation
does not come in a risk-free environment —

if God has delegated his authority
to a team of editors and correspondents

in different times and languages, is it
surprising that his trust should be repaid

with anomalies and factual mistakes? Even prophets
must be given freedom to be wrong.

18

It would be hard to get the New Testament
    convicted
on a charge of apostolic authority. Out of

nine or ten writers — not including Q —
four at most heard Jesus' promise

in the upper room, that "when the Spirit comes
he will guide you into all truth." The synoptics

all drew on unattributed pool reports, the Gentile
Luke took the whole thing down second-hand; Paul,

well we have his word for his apostleship —
in whatever sense you like — but who will vouch

for Mark? James? Jude? 2 Peter? Or could
    even guess
the writer to the Hebrews? I don't doubt

their inspiration, Andrew, but the doctrine's flawed,
no wise house could now be founded on such sand.

19

The Jews I think say there are
three meanings for anything in the Torah —

the plain sense, the prophetic
and the hidden, real significance — well, it's true

that Matthew's use of Scripture wouldn't last
five minutes in a sound Evangelical school!

In this debate at least, Andrew,
it's time that we put down this mongrel reason,

born out of Aristotle and Descartes,
cross-bred with Darwin, Freud and Jung —

slipping the leash of faith it has turned wild,
this pit-bull logic, with the jaws

of its *reductio ad absurdum* locked
on anything that might get in its way.

20

God had the choice of technologies. We could have
    received
the perfect, unambiguous written Word,

no missing Hebrew vowels or doubtful
readings, no variant manuscripts, disputed
    authorship —

the letters clearly signed by Paul or John
(or maybe Barnabas) — translated into

every language, with second copies placed
in safe deposit in case of accidents:

but this way he has given us his commandments
without tripping us up at the first —

or should we seek out some Aaron to re-cast
the golden idol of inerrancy,

and set it up and worship it amongst
the anachronistic stones of Jericho and Ai?

21

Who sanctions this search
for a systematic theology? Christ,

who talked in parables? Only God
could reconcile the strains of these

scholastic gymnastics, and knowing faith to be
more powerful than certainty

he chooses to do something else instead. Just as
his image persists within our sinfulness

so truth inhabits our ambiguous language, truth
that is not the whole truth,

and rarely nothing but the truth, that
in a fallen world can only be displayed

in an imperfect medium, and in its revelation
puts dogma on the rack, where it belongs.

22

Imagine one more myth. Suppose there was
an image, once, of perfect truth,

in which Adam looked, until like everything
it was shattered in the Fall, its pieces strewn

across the centuries. Most came to rest
in a small, untidy, squabbled-over country,

where men, by diligence or what seemed luck,
discovered fragments, stained or brightly polished,
    edges

sharp enough to wound; they swept up sixty-six,
each one a book, and when with careful restoration

at Nicaea they had done the best they could
they held it up at last — the Bible, Paul's dark glass,

a broken mirror that somehow returns
the cracked reflection of the face of God.

23

We do not find God by theology
nor coax him out of hiding with our worship.

We discover him instead
in places that we least expect, where his power

is concealed by insignificance: in the little
act of kindness seeking no reward,

the momentary thought for others, obedience
in a thing thought trivial — matters

so small they are like
a medicine of such a weak solution

as to be hardly there at all, and traceable
by no known science — yet these are

our real investments, the widow's mites with which
he finances his kingdom's public spending.

24

That he should choose obscurity
comes as no surprise — the Jewish books

are testaments of the implausible,
their heroes a cast of rejects: Abraham

and his ancient, sterile wife;
the upstart Jacob; Moses, doubly an outcast;

Rahab the scheming prostitute; Gideon the feeble;
David the overlooked son; Ruth, widow, foreigner,

woman; and all the ragged conscripts of the
    prophets;
the divine script is the story of the blessed
    underdog —

even the chosen people themselves, a nation
of such global unimportance that successive
    conquerors

allowed them to continue in the worship
of their quaint, invisible and plainly harmless God.

25

The history of Israel is a black cloak of failure
patched with brief colours of brighter cloth —

covenants broken, the pointless
wandering in the desert,

anarchy under judges and the tragedy of kings:
Saul's madness, David's lechery,

Solomon and all his wives, and after them
the slow descent into apostasy,

dogs kept off by alliances with wolves,
Jerusalem defiled, ransacked, abandoned,

then painfully and partially restored —
if it seems familiar it is because it is

our own story, the tale of good intent
sacrificed to the idols of our selves.

26

From his first word
God's efforts to communicate hardly ceased.

His choice of media was comprehensive:
earthquakes, winds, floods, fires, still small voices,

burning bushes, tablets, parables,
plumblines, angels, donkeys, plagues and dreams,

potters' wheels, handwriting on the wall,
the quiet chat in the desert, the mass

meeting for the reading of the Law,
and then for five hundred years

pouring out through prophet after prophet
pleadings and promises and dire warnings

that bordered on despair — in all of this
the message never changed: return, be healed.

27

Finally it seemed God had given them up
and for four centuries there was no word,

just the crushing weight of military occupations,
like a dowry for this nation

that had married once too often
with foreign gods; in the Judaean hills

the Maccabeans chose out their Messiahs
and shook their swords at heaven for its silence.

But all this time God was gathering his breath
to speak his last tremendous word,

and when it was delivered
it was squeezed out from a single human body

in the only, painful way there is and laid out
helpless, derelict and in the heart of nowhere.

28

The word said "Become like this
or you will never find me —

if you are simple you will hear angels,
if you are wise you must watch for signs

and both will lead you to bring your questions
and lay them at this improbable manger

where I have placed the passion
that will consume all of mankind. This is what I
    mean

when I say the kingdom of heaven
is like a mustard seed, that it is

folly to the wise and a stone on which
the righteous will stumble, for I have not come

for the righteous, of whom there are none,
but to save sinners, of whom there are already
    enough."

29

The word was squeezed out like a drop
of ointment, a single spot

of water in the desert, or the first
tiny crack in the fault before an earthquake; the
    word was

a whisper barely audible, but in the hollow
of our hearts it echoed, and the echo grew

to a sound that made the whole world
stop its ears in case its ringing should crack

the deep glazing of our self-satisfaction and into
our earthen vessels pour its treasure. The word

broke in like a visitation of angels,
its bright light scattering the thin

flocks of our achievements that we graze
so carefully in high, unfriendly pastures.

30

"Fear not" the herald said — yet until then
I think the shepherds were quite unconcerned —

cold, perhaps, or quarrelsome, or bored, but not
expecting anything to happen, and anxious

only for the usual domestic reasons. What scared
    them
was the sight of their clean, familiar sky ripped open

by beings from another dimension,
brilliant with the news that God

has become a man, and is quite unlike
anything that we expected — this is something

to be afraid of, Andrew, this rude
intrusion into the world we thought we had created:

the owner has turned burglar, breaking in
to steal our Chubb-locked hearts, and throw the
    keys away.

31

The ark sailed backwards through the centuries
beyond the reach of modern scholarship: Einstein

discovered nothing to which it was related, Galileo
failed to trace its course in the stars, da Vinci

could only speculate on its design, Columbus
was the boldest, with the least successful result —

and when it was found at last,
by the shepherds acting on a tip-off,

it was much smaller than we had imagined, just
a wooden box, with a few beasts attending,

hardly adequate, you'd think, for the deliverance
of all humanity from the flood of judgement,

its single occupant asleep, and over all the covenant
    sign,
not a rainbow but Golgotha, the soul's true Ararat.

32

This was no rehearsal. Failure was possible
but he could not fail — his strength

became his weakness, for he knew
the power of unlimited temptation

but not the luxury of giving in; he met
human kind in its squalor and brutality

and took exception only to its pride.
And our lives are no rehearsal: unlike

the Irishman giving directions we can't say
"I wouldn't start from here"— he

won't wait for us to become respectable
but finds us, like Zacchaeus, up a gum tree

or the woman in her well of promiscuity, places
    where
we can hardly bear his failure to be shocked.

33

The Bible says Jesus loved Lazarus so much
that, hearing he was ill, he stayed away

just long enough for him to die. The sisters'
grief turned to anger and confusion, knowing

that it need not have been so — Mary
fell at his feet with a sullen

ignorant rebuke: "Lord, if you had been here . . . "
And we are Mary. Her four days' despair

has been drawn out in us for two millennia,
the word we sent remains unanswered while

those that are loved go to their certain
deaths — He will come again

when it all seems much too late, shouting
"Come out" to a bound and stinking world.

34

These poems should have been about the cross,
    Andrew,
but who could do that? We, who wait here

in its long shadow, trying to look up
and unable, knowing that to gaze directly at it

will burn out the pupils of our self-esteem? It is not
finished: that face (R S Thomas said it) is "staring

as over twenty centuries it has stared,
from unfathomable darkness into unfathomable
    light",

while we between both look on, helpless
like children in Dickens, bewildered heirs

to some great estate, watching
the tragic tale unfold, knowing

our future joy depends on this transaction
in whose genesis we are somehow implicated.

35

Put down this bag of words,
coins for a potter's field. Whose

likeness do they bear? God is diminished
by all our explanations: we have made

Christ in our own image, scourged him
with the whips of our doctrines, wrapped

his beaten body in our purple prose,
frozen his agony in window glass

and made the cross a trinket. In all we know
there is no analogue for Calvary:

but for three hours on a Friday afternoon
Jerusalem lay in unearthly darkness

while on a scaffold the eternal word
hung silent, staring, gape-mouthed, perfectly dead.

36

This is where faith begins,
not during some religious palaver

when our thoughts are on their Sunday best
    behaviour,
but at a rubbish tip outside a city. Three figures

approach a fourth sitting alone, and the huge
silence of the ancient world is pierced

by Job's unintelligible howl of pain, the cry
of faithful ignorance, the unanswerable question

"Why have you forsaken me?" hanging in the air
for its answering echo, a thousand years later

from another rubbish tip outside another city. This is
the place of sacrifice to which we bring

our most-cherished theories, caught like Isaac's ram
in the impenetrable thicket of good and evil.

37

We move with a certain grace, like skaters
going quickly on the thin ice

of our lives and theology, afraid
of what might happen if we stop too long

to contemplate the depths beneath. This
picture, drawn by a dying woman, pulls apart

the brittle surface of our lives to show
the gaps in our broken world let in no darkness,

but the light that always shines
unseen behind it; its jagged

border frames the outline of a body
created purely out of pain; and that

the pieces of our lives are held in place
by what so often looks just like his absence.

38

For what is it we pray? That peace
will come, and prophecy go unfulfilled?

For the unchangeable to change his mind?
In a game of blind man's buff

beneath the storms of God we hide
or lay out the tarpaulin of our prayers

and catch what grace we can, asking
"that it will not be in winter",

and though our intercessions seem as futile
as five small loaves among five thousand men,

he breaks the bread of our prayers
to feed the hungry who come

to eat, gathered so far out
at the edge of the soul's miraculous hillside.

39

I'm no raving charismatic (as you know!)
but what dogma brings you — David Watson's
        curate —

to say some gifts are not
for us here and today? What then

are these signs? Wishful thinking?
Something worse? Would you confine

his supernatural utterances to one time and place,
say that the God of Job is bound

to speak now only after proper exegesis? Andrew,
in God's supreme untidiness I only see

he will do what he wants to when he wants to,
and speak in whatever tongue or form of silence

best suits his purpose to confound
our stolid pharasaic study of divine behaviour.

40

Our African friend Kenneth says
his church depends on spiritual power

because they've no money for medicines.
Our sceptical analysis is nothing more

than the reasoning of the rich, who have placed
their faith in the NHS and BUPA

to insure against such acts of God.
These healings are

like early blossom of a coming summer:
this is his nursing love, to ease

the symptoms of a dying world, where health
is a mercy and not a right; and where although

the antidote was given long ago, it still appears
sin's virulence must run its bloody course.

41

For two thousand years
we seem to have got it wrong — the cherished

wisdom of one century becomes
anathema to the next. God

is someone immeasurably greater
than we might conceive, who does not need

all our apologetics and leaves us just
the truth that we can bear.

These brooding contradictions are our guides
through the doorway of salvation,

and somewhere out of time the whole
unjust distribution of resources

will be safely gathered up — Tessa once said
the plural of paradox must be paradise.

42

You won't take offence at this, I'm sure,
from one who "hides God's counsel without
    knowledge"!

Out of the mental whirlwind he still speaks
the words of eternal life — humble,

unanswerable. Heaven's wonders are not learned
in any college or debate, but in

our everyday endurance where we gain
the few things that are needful: faith

that will outstare the frozen gaze of logic;
hope that hangs on when sense is beaten; love

that fashions out of human anguish
the material of eternity — these three remain,

and Corrie ten Boom's words, "the closer you get to
    God
the less you understand, the more believe."

43

A friend gave me this picture,
that like Ezekiel's river from the temple

the clear torrent of the Spirit pours down
the stony channels of our enterprise

and all our arguments amount
to a few old rusty implements, blunt shears and
     rakes

stuck in the river bed, and of no more use
than knives to slice waves from a waterfall. Here

in the sunny silence of a winter afternoon
outside this upper room the trees stretch out

as if in supplication. These words are scattered
in the valley of dry bones, waiting

for the rustling of the wind of God, waiting
for the coming spring, the breath of Pentecost.

44

Eleven thirty. Tessa lies with eyes closed
fighting a fever, mine open at my book wrestling

with the Welsh priest-poet's images of God.
The little girl comes in, her pale face

serious: "I want a cuddle"— she wriggles
down into the gap between us. "Did you have

a bad dream?" "Yes." "What was it about?"
"I don't know." She lies there still, the warmth

of our closeness all the comforting she needs.
And I don't know what it was about,

the guilt, the bargaining, all that wasted time
spent second-guessing God: the Father loves us

as I love Emma and Joel — not because
they're good or clever, but because they're mine.

45

I remember how one night some years ago,
driving alone on the M25, I saw

a 747 blinking in the sky and thought of you
flying back from America, those dreams

broken like stubborn heresies, your seeming failure
broadcast to those who love you,

Kate and Charlotte a consolation, with all
your fragile certainties intact and still

convinced of our gift for sin. The lights
of Heathrow beckoned someone home — it might

be you or me up there in all that darkness,
aching for landing, locked into that beam

as keen as radar, drawing us slowly down
in endless circles, moths to His great flame.